About the Author

Based in London, Sara Disalvo works mainly as a
Wellbeing Practitioner with young people and families. She
works both on a one-to-one basis and runs workshops and
webinars as part of the offer. Alongside this, she runs her
private counselling practice, working with adults, young
people and couples. She also has experience in teaching
counselling courses, something she is currently taking a
break from due to daily work commitments. She is very
fortunate as she loves her work and life itself, always
seeking new ventures and experiences. Life balance is very
important for her, so even though she works very hard, time
with her immediate family and friends is essential. She also
loves spending time with her dog, they can often be found
walking on the beach or a country park somewhere. Or
having a glass of wine and dinner in the pub.

Be Brave

Sara Disalvo

Be Brave

Olympia Publishers
London

www.olympiapublishers.com
OLYMPIA PAPERBACK EDITION

A CIP catalogue record for this title is
available from the British Library.

ISBN: 978-1-80074-982-5

First Published in 2023

Olympia Publishers
Tallis House
2 Tallis Street
London
EC4Y 0AB

Printed in Great Britain

Dedication

I dedicate this book to my daughters, Jasmine and Madeline.

Acknowledgements

This book was written out of my life experiences, it could not have been written if I had not been alive. I would like to thank everyone who has crossed my path, the good, the challenging, the inspiring and the damaging. You see, without every single experience, I would not have been able to live and learn to facilitate my life change. Thank you all.

Introduction

Writing these diary entries helped me manage my dark days and gave me joy on the more uplifting moments. It was never my intention for these words to be made into a book, as I was not ever going to write one.

Waking one day, I had the urge to put pen to paper. Every paragraph was emotionally driven, every word the raw truth of my feelings that day. I began to enjoy writing; it gave me focus and was something to read over and to reflect on and learn from. My thinking that if I could learn from my story then maybe some others could too, or at least get some comfort from what they read.

At times of woe, you start looking around for comfort, something that will help you get through. I could not find anything that mirrored where I was, what I was going through. Instead, I took wise words from many great people and started to piece my own theoretical approach and a way forward. Everyone has advice and an opinion, I had to keep strong and rely on my gut feeling, what did I feel was right?

With no plan or structure to what I was about to do I remember laying in my bed after the worst night's sleep ever thinking how I was going to take this forward, feeling like I was starting life again but this time I was in the driving seat. As I mention, my gut told me I would be okay; however, not knowing how I was to do that. The loss I was feeling weighed heavy on me. I knew one thing – I had to go it alone this time, push everyone away. I needed to be able to hear my inner voice. You can't do that when everyone is talking around you. Sure, I would listen to friendly advice, but I was now making my decisions. The realisation that I had never lived my life I was always living others' lives, them being my focus.

I had no choice, no matter what happened I did not ever want to go back, I had seen the crack in the door and made a run for it, never knowing what was on the other side.

Looking back on the most painful days when I would sit and beg for them to stop and the daily pain I endured to go away, I realise each one of them was necessary. My theory is that where there is pain there is potential growth, if you are prepared to learn from it. It has led me to feel stronger and more grounded than I ever have. Does that mean I will not make mistakes and trip over? Hell no. I am a human being; my default position is to fuck up! However, I have learned to get up quicker and recover. Mostly now living in a responsive state.

When writing this, the negative thought flashes into my awareness. "Get a grip – your problems are nowhere near as bad as others'". Clients say this all the time, they feel bad for reflecting on feelings they have and compare. I always tell them that our suffering is our own, we cannot measure it, it is all relative. So, I am going to boldly say, sure for onlookers this may not seem like a life tragedy, however, I am going to own my pain and suffering I went through and accept it instead of comparing it.

At the time of my life re-launch, I was going through a divorce, which is a main focal point of the text. However, my message to you is that this book could be applied to many different life situations. You do not have to be divorced or considering divorce to appreciate my story. This is a story about a turn in life and finally being true to myself.

At nearly fifty I decided enough was enough, to find my peace I needed to take time out and be alone. With no plan I made an overnight decision to change everything and follow my gut feeling. Not knowing where life would take me or how any of this would look. I took a leap of faith closed my eyes and jumped.

So... where am I now? I don't really recognise my life, I believed in what I could create, I am in an emotionally stable state. My life is my own, I make my decisions, I am free. The 'Being Brave' is something I remind myself of almost daily. It would be easy now to settle with what I have, and of course that would be okay. However, I want to keep moving as life has much more to offer me, of this, I am sure.

Change can be addictive, especially when you no longer fear it, so the danger is to change for change's sake. As with all aspects of life there is a balance there that I need to master. The way I feel is that I could up sticks and keep changing. Going forward I need to keep this measured. I will ask myself why I am making the change and what would be my gain?

What I have taken away from this adventure is that to bring about change I had to focus on changing and to make it work for me. I had to be courageous, fear stops us changing and growing, we limit ourselves, we must learn to push through with a positive message. Allow and appreciate change, no limitations, remember you are your own limitation.

I would encourage people to make the changes as it gets easier once you have become accustomed to it. Be brave and embrace change.

Blank Paper

So, I seem to have been given a rather large blank piece of paper representing my life ahead. I guess I am exaggerating slightly; some things are still on that paper. Myself and my children... that is all that I can think of that is fixed, the rest is up to me. What do I now want to see in front of me? My children's future on the paper but now they have their own lives ahead of them with their own pieces of paper. So, I am all that is left, standing at the very edge looking forward but not sure of the direction I will take.

Excited, impatient, a little worried? Not really, worried is what others are projecting on to me. Worried is not something I exactly feel, you see I have always had this feeling right in the pit of my stomach that I predominately will be okay. Life will look after me, sure life will throw mud, but I will always recover. I will also have times when I wonder what this is all about, but you see I love life and all it has to offer. My default position is one of excitement and enthusiasm for what lays ahead; there is always something out there for me just around the corner. Not sure if that is fixed destiny or that I will make it all happen.

Realising that deep down I ride through life on my unicorn, full of the romantic dream life could offer me, is it now time to get off? Hell no, I want to keep riding at a fast speed, why get off now? This is the part where life could explode, I know, it could also go way down hill and I could be miserable for ever more. Damn that negative voice, again not what I believe. Guess what? My life will not be miserable, I am at the centre of my life, and I hold the ability to make myself happy. Done it before and can do it again. All I need to work out is what components make a person happy? More so what will work for me now?

I always wanted the dream and more, unable to settle for life's normal, done that, been there. It was good to be grounded for a while even sensible but now I need new adventures, some excitement and to meet new people to start loading my half full cup up once more. Life told me to conform, I have fitted into other people's normal, that is not really who I am, big question that one. Who are you? Yes, we have all stopped and asked ourselves that question at some point. If you have not, then maybe it is time to get started now. Are you fitting into social norms, others' expectations? Making the huge decision to write my own script from now on and to live from that as much as possible, I pause, the blank paper flashes before my eyes once more. Stopping to think about that, there is always interference from other script writers, with you staring in as the character they want to see. You see, if you fit their script, it enables them to continue with their safe story. As soon as you erase yourself and re-enter yourself as a different character everything starts to rock. Whether I am changing or just presenting it is making those around me respond differently. Some confessing to their own life tragedies, others communicating freely as I have let my own guard down.

Working out this equation may take me a while; I have decided to plot things on the paper, with me at the bottom of the page looking ahead. Once thinking that I was climbing to the top of Maslow's hierarchy pyramid I now find myself at the bottom again trying to figure out how to build those foundation blocks.

The only certain thing in life is uncertainty, this was said to me in the initial stages of my turn. With a foot note that the only certain thing was that I would at some point be deceased. Hoping that this would not be soon as I had far too much to do. Seriously, how true this was. We spend far too much time worrying about everything when as I have found out at the flip of a coin whether self-inflicted or not life can change in an instant. This plays nicely into my new life theory, why worry? Or to be more explicit: Fuck it. Fuck it, fuck it, and fuck it. This is my new favourite phrase; it feels empowering to say it and more to act it out.

I have spent far too much time worrying about stuff that just does not matter. The saying "Don't sweat the small stuff" never far from my thoughts.

At this moment I am deliberating on what will be the next, things getting me through the day are, work, solitude, talking to my extended group and listening to music, oh and the gym. After advocating the balance between mind and body for so long, I am listening to my own advice. Suddenly I am also listening to every lyric in every song, making that connection with what is being sung. The effect? Happiness, anger, sadness but mostly reflection and creativity. Nothing like a life changing event to get the creative juices flowing. Feelings that are going to make me burst. It is like I have suddenly turned into a balloon that is expanding with feelings and thoughts and excitement and a tinge of sadness for what is about to pass. There is something else out there for me, just waiting.

Impatience, if this has taught me anything it is patience with a big capital P. I am so ready for the next chapter, but guess what? Divine time has stepped in my way. The balloon I talk about is a huge holding bay for all I am thinking and feeling right now. Floating around in this balloon, hoping it does not burst or if it does it is because my life is going to explode rather than burst, deflate. Negative thought again, almost like I must balance the positive with a negative just in case. Is this realism or only plain old pessimism? Never quite sure where the line is drawn between the two. The question has been asked, 'Is she having a nervous breakdown?' No, she is definitely not. Yes, she is going through life changing feelings, acting a little crazy, huge highs and lows but mostly just spending time working out, what next? With Rome not being built in a day, I expect I need to have my good friend patience. Surely laced with fun somewhere to see me through.

I guess I need to explain a couple of things. I am a therapist, separated from my husband awaiting divorce and the mother to my two girls, whom I love more than life itself. Also separated from my family through choice, guess that is debatable. Really going it alone for the first time, everything I know is about to change.

Then the crash, the bereavement has washed over me. So much of my life that I had pushed to one side and not dealt with just crashed in on me. Need to mentally take time to work through it all and sort it back into boxes, putting them away when reflected on. Whilst all the time being on this emotional rollercoaster of feelings. Laughter, sadness, happiness, to name a few.

After a short conversation about counselling training last week with a colleague and voicing my opinion that you do not get the best out of people if you put them in a corner, the other therapist replied that she agreed and that, "We are all wounded." Hearing those words made me stop; I kept repeating it to myself on the journey home. How did I feel knowing that she was right? As therapists we are all wounded in some way to varying degrees of course.

Maybe for the first time it felt okay to say, "Yes, I have been wounded and I have been attempting to heal those wounded parts of myself. After all I am inviting my clients to do the same, step forward and repair or at least acknowledge those wounded parts. I have been re connecting with my adolescent self, revisiting who I was back then and what I stood for before life took me over."

Whilst at university yesterday we visited humanistic approaches and as I have stated before the Rogerian theoretical approach is featuring much more in my life and work. When asked by the lecturer why that was, I explained that I was going through a major life change/divorce and that I was now focusing for the first time on my own inner voice and internal locus of evaluation, how I really feel about life. My views have always been strong but over the years I have learnt to dampen them down through fear of not fitting in or my views not being understood. That theme continues today but I am now prepared to own my thoughts and feelings and express them. The strongest part and the underpinning of my work is that we all have potential for change, and even though you may have been labelled bad or made mistakes that are following you around, it is not too late to take another path or do something different. I can offer you a non-judgmental space to explore what your inner voice is saying in a world where you are led by the adult voices around you. Bad behaviour does not automatically mean bad person, there is need to separate the person from the behaviour. This does not equate to a boundary less existent, far from it, just the luxury of a space to explore what else is on offer. My inner teenager also seems to want to be explored, helped through the work I am completing. So needed to talk to someone back then.

My Divorce

In the eyes of the law, I have been unreasonable and really have no issue with taking that responsibility. My belief is that you should be able to divorce, no one having to be blamed. I believe this is currently being looked at, let us hope this law is passed soon. Growing apart and not loving someone any more does not seem to 'cut the mustard'. Society likes playing the blame game; we must hold someone somewhere accountable. I am quite certain that portioning the blame to one of the parties has the potential to cause more upset and conflict, time for change.

So, having pressed the red button I am now going ahead and facing the biggest part of this whole situation. I am a little sad in what I am turning my back on, I feel myself glancing over my shoulder with tears in my eyes and then looking forward with nothing but uncertainty, tinged with hope. The safety blanket of my family home and my marriage is slowly slipping away, due to me letting go bit by bit. It is almost like having a bit of an out of body experience, I am really doing this. Is this becoming a reality? We are capable of so much more than we give ourselves credit for, a tough road but possible.

7 November, 2017

In a strange place, neither happy nor sad. Feel more even and able to cope with the day ahead. Almost like there is no base feeling but my thoughts are still overactive. Not sure how to combat that. There have been some glimpses of happiness over the past week, some great experiences then I come back to base. I guess it brings me back to be patient again which is hard as I am so clear on what I want but not sure if it wants me! Am I in another temporary space? Suddenly wanting to know what my future looks like, where is this all leading me too? I need to enjoy the good and the glimmers of happy when they come and then be prepared to let go again.

My work helps, being busy and having another focus. Wow, how inward I have become – me, me, and me. Never thought about me so much, being on your own with your own thoughts gives you clarity and space to receive.

13 November, 2017

Had to give myself a pep talk this morning, was that just because it was the dreaded Monday? Just have to get through today and then I will be okay? Reminding myself that I have a lot to be thankful for, and that everything is going to be okay. Slight anxiety but trying to bat that away and practice mindfulness. Just deal with the day ahead, no use projecting into the future. How many times will I have to tell myself that? It is like I am stupid; I repeat the same stuff every week, and most of what I have to say comes true. After all I have survived the past five months have I not? Even had some glimmers of happiness, fun times, enlightening moments. I AM NOT UNHAPPY. This is just about change, yes, I have got to be patient, but I will get there, wherever that is. Still no master plan but it is still full steam ahead.

So, I decided that I would give social media a try. It has already been positive. Back in touch with my tutor who was inspirational to all of us at school. I would even go as far as a kindred spirit. She has invited me to visit to catch up, we both feel we need to speak to one another. I am a half empty cup that is now having new experiences that are filling my cup up once more. I am trying to go with the flow and get others input into what the hell life is all about. I feel very alone in my quest as I do not have any one that really understands what it is, I am doing. My supervisor would get it, I will update her soon.

20 November, 2017

A feeling of calm has washed over me, feeling very peaceful and has been for quite a few days. Had forgotten what it felt like as my feelings have been a little out of control over the past five months. Almost feeling back to a place of normality but slightly different. Keep centring myself when I feel like a runaway train. Bringing the feelings back in and talking to me, telling me that everything is okay. Practising Cognitive Behavioural Therapy, repeating the same things until it sinks inward.

Realising that I am forty-five and have never flown on my own; I have decided to take my first solo flight tomorrow, a little apprehensive but also excited to spend some time on my own. Looking forward to the flight, just sitting and having some reflection time. Time just for me to do what I want for a couple of days. Sun, sun, sun, here I come! The difference being away from home is that you have no boring chores to do, just time to yourself. I want to swim, relax in the sun and eat and drink. Saying that makes me just want to close my eyes.

Peaceful, that is the feeling I have. I have realised that as humans we can endure a fair amount of life happening to ourselves, yes, it is tough going through it, but we are more resilient that we imagine. The more we go through the more resilient we become. This changes us and affects our work and the way we are with others. It is making me gentler in my approach, less black and white, less dramatic about life in general, more understanding about the human condition. As much as it is a cliché, my girls are my inspiration in their very separate way. I fill up with tears at the mere thought of them both. They have carried me through in so many ways. Lifted my spirits and basically are the loves of my life. I am only sorry that I could not have provided them with more in life. I have tried my best throughout. I hope it has been enough.

28 November 2017

Once more bursting with creativity and an amalgamation of feelings I need to express. Riding on a cloud of happiness today, never imagined I would ever feel or experience this again or ever.

Already achieving so much in small ways, realisation that 'this girl can', no denying it has been six months of ups and downs and no reason to believe that there will not be more. My primary focus for the first time in my life has been me. I have had my full concentration, is this what is meant when they talk about self-care? If it is then it feels good, after all I could not keep giving, without taking this time to fix myself and make a promise to myself that this will be an ongoing feature. Still a hell of a mountain to climb but aware that you never know what you are capable of until you go through life's events. I do not need to know where this is heading now, that is no longer my primary focus instead I am just focusing on the week's events. That way I can cope with it all.

Still practising positive thinking, and mindfulness with CBT techniques. This has had a knock-on effect to my work. I am really engaged with all that I am doing especially my teaching, I am getting so much out of every individual in that room.

I am thankful for such a lot in my life. Learning to appreciate and look at the positive rather than the negatives. I am a believer in sending out positivity and therefore getting it back.

So, what has changed? Everything and nothing, I guess. I really believe that I am getting back to who I was and got lost in everyone else's conditions of worth. I constantly ask myself the question what Sara thinks about that. No longer willing to live the way others expect me to, far too fun-loving for that. Need for the balance in life working hard, quite a serious affair then fun and some happiness to balance it out. My change is not without challenges, but I believe in all that I am doing so will follow my gut feeling. I know deep down!

Like a bird caged I did not fly
Like a caged bird confined to your space
I let you all make me believe I had to stay
In that little space conforming to
Realisation of how I can be
Who I want, what I see?
My wings were clipped, I flew so far

Was made to believe I had to stay
This bright blue bird has spread its wings and left the cage
Flying solo, trying new things
Seeing how it all feels, like the first time
Not sure where it will fly to now it has been let free.

Do not make the mistake of thinking I will stay in one of your boxes
I am free to fly, why, why, why
Do not make mistake my feelings as a trap to keep me
I am free to fly
You have trapped yourself, confined to one of your boxes
I am free to fly

Frustrated, confined trying to break out
Do I end it or follow it through?
Is this a test of patience, are my feelings true?
I have feelings that are strong, too strong to turn away.
I know how I feel what I want but no chance of letting him know
Do I take a chance or save myself now?
Turn around walk away, or simply stay.
Teardrops falling, oh why am I sad
I feel like crying feeling oh so sad
Yesterday I was ecstatic, so what has changed?
What I feel what I have heard what has changed.
I am feeling lonely, no one to share
My feelings I want to lay bare.
Who could possibly understand what I am going

through?

A massive change, a U-turn, and feelings I need to spare
Anxiety, happiness, sad all in a day
My happiness of yesterday has gone away.
Hearing your sad stories some day's hard to contain.
You share I listen, your sadness I hold.
I look at you, your loss, your pain yet you are getting on.

Christmas is approaching, kill me now. Cannot cope with it, don't want it so what do I do? 'Hide away,' is my first thought. 'Escape, run away.' But I guess I need to face it and deal with my fate.

So, this weekend I will take a deep breath, take charge and drive this ship forward. It will all be over soon!

Sadness today, realise it is because it is my baby's seventeenth birthday. Love her so much and just want her to have a great birthday but know it is going to be hard for her and that I am to blame for her upset, does not make me feel great. Trying to contain the way I feel and not let it spill over into all the other aspects of my life. It is hard today, reached out to a friend who understood; just want to spend the day crying.

Self-care, I have no idea what that looks like really. Here I am pretending I am doing the whole self-care thing when really, I am far from it.

Woke up this morning crying, a huge feeling of wanting to just lay on the floor and someone take care of my emotional needs, because that has never happened.

For the first time ever, I want to feel what it is like to have someone there for me emotionally, sure I have lots of amazing supportive friends who have been there for me and would be more if I let them. Why do I do it, do not want to seem weak or needy or vulnerable. I am vulnerable, and I do have needs that one day I would like meeting. I have proved to the world I can be independent; take care of me and those around me. I am now exhausted, this needs to stop now, I can no longer sell my soul.

17 February, 2018

I have come so far on my journey, faced up to a lot of my fears, come to some huge realisations about myself and realised there is so much more to fix. Now I can say out loud for the first time I am scared, frightened and that I need help. That makes me vulnerable as in my mind I am leaving myself wide open for others to take advantage of the way I feel. I have been described as strong and maybe now I want to display the vulnerable part of me, let others know that it is okay to feel this way; to say to myself. "It is okay to feel scared." If I am really going to move forward then I need to get it all out, no pretence. Right now, I just want to curl up and cry, feeling like it is difficult to function now. Want to give up and say enough is enough, I can't do this anymore, the road is just too damn tough. Of course, I will not give up as I will not be defeated but I am going to allow myself day's where I am knocked down. We sometimes fill up on too much positivity, having other feelings is okay too. I need to be thankful for all the experiences that are put my way good and the not so good as they will all go into the filling up of my big cup.

Closing my eyes and jumping, there are no certainties ahead, no master plans I am acting on how I feel. Do not want to turn back; instinctively know there is life ahead, something better to come but no absolute. I cannot have what I want right at this moment as I do not think I really know yet. Or correction, I have my wants, the wants that will temporarily pacify me but as my outlook changes weekly how can I know what the picture looks long term. So, the part I wrangle with is temporary situations, are they okay? The quick pleasure, the, 'This is okay for now but will not serve me long term.' You see all the messages I received growing up were about long-term goals, relationships, jobs and just sticking with things for what seemed like forever. Now I am trying to adapt myself into someone who can do temporary, as this is the space, I find myself in. Not quite at my destination, neither at the start therefore trying to live for the day, week or month even. In a weird way I do not want to put myself on hold as I may not reach my destination for some time, I still need to live in the meanwhile and have experiences to take me forward. The conclusion I have come to is sure have your temporary experiences if they do not distract from your destination (unknown) or side-track you from your development.

21st February, 2018

Reflecting on how far I have come in the last eight months I concluded that physical change has happened however, the biggest mountain climbed is my state of mind. Having allowed myself this time to be by myself and indulge in self-thought. Fundamentally my main structure of ideas has not changed but as I develop the smaller details are not so clear. What I mean by this is yes, I want the divorce and to live on my own, expand my work but I am more open minded to where I might live and what the future may look like. Happier to go with the flow of life, the urgencies to be in a fixed position are no longer a priority. Trying to enjoy this transition without the focus on the end picture, after all who is to say that I may not be transitioning for quite some time? So why should I not try to enjoy the journey there. As I previously have talked about living with the temporary does not have to be unhappy and chaotic as I first imagined, as in reality we only have this moment in time anyway.

Attachment is the word that springs to mind, my attachment style is secure **(Bowlby)**. I make fixed secure attachments with people. Never been a people collector in any way and the fact was pointed out to me that when pushed I can cut people off. Not in a cold way but I seem to have the ability to cut and move on when something has run its course, I guess that is also feeling secure and having a secure base that has allowed me to do that. The question on my mind is, 'Does being on your own still allow that secure base to operate from or do you need another to co-create that base?' I have to say, I still feel secure now, but I am still living in a slight bubble. It will be interesting to explore how this affects me going forward.

23rd February, 2018
Divorce, I am avoiding it no more. Sure, I have talked about it as if I were about to do something about it but then avoided it once more. I made the lawyer laugh yesterday as I confessed to having referred others to her over the last few months without attending my own appointment. Again, it was fear that kept me away and that without stating the obvious it is such a final act. During the day, my nerves got

the better of me and I nearly cancelled again.

A huge relief is the only way to describe my feeling after leaving the appointment. Methodically she went through it all in a very user-friendly way, literately step by step. I now feel I have regained some confidence to continue going forward, as agreed in a hopefully friendly manner. That is my hope, and it is a big ask but I hope we can be as amicable as possible. I would say that as it is me that wants it yes, but I have no interest in causing any one any more distress than need be. It has also given me an image of what my future may look like.

I now find myself writing three to four paragraphs on my unreasonable behaviour! As I am going to be the respondent and he the petitioner. Basically, taking responsibility for the breakdown of the marriage and being cited as displaying unreasonable behaviour.

Relationships

20th February, 2018

Whilst listening to a mixture of songs on a rainy drive into school this morning, I started thinking about the complexity of the relationships we have in our everyday lives. This is due to each of the lyrics telling me a slightly different story. Getting me to think about this subject, of course the other factor was the way I was feeling this morning. My own relationships all up for consideration. Family issues, marriage separation and changing friendships all leading me to consider which relationships I wanted, and in which form. Also, potential new relationships that may be out there, with life experience behind me, surely, I would want something different. Desperately trying not to fall into the same patterns. Would I be able to do something different, be different, and have what I now needed? Deciding now that I would work from a script, I was writing myself not the script of ancestors, friends and acquaintances.

I have changed. Now I have realised the need for something is those around me have the chance to adjust. The one thing I have noted is that as I become more open about what is going on for me, those around let their defences down and are more open with the reality of their own relationships.

The overriding single factor that stayed in my mind was the fact that as individuals we all want different things, it is just a matter of finding others that want the same. I guess later in life I would want something different to the past relationships. Having changed now have realised the need something a little more progressive. Firstly, having my emotion needs met. This realisation has been brought to my attention quite recently. Obviously, you need to explore what your needs are first.

Questioning, looking at other relationships listening to what is being said, all impacting on my thought process around the relationship debate. Is there a right or wrong in relationships? Should they not be a little more bespoke? Do we just settle for the social norm? I see lots of unhappy, unhealthy relationships where couples just put up with it all. I believe in working at relationships in general but not to the extent of unhappiness of one or both parties. So why do we continue to stay...

We do not feel the same or hopefully remain the same as people for forty years so why would we expect our relationships to? We need different things from life at different times that now seems obvious.

Laughter, being made to laugh is so important, it is an important aspect, connection and warmth. Communication is key, cannot say it enough. What prevents us from saying what it is we really feel? Rejection, judgement or that we just do not want to talk to them anymore, we no longer want that connection with that person.

Healthy relationships, somewhere you meet adult to adult and connect with one another. Taking it a step further I want a soul connection, that much deeper understating on a level far away from the surface. Still keeping your independence but the ability to be in tune with the other's needs and desires.

6 March, 2018

Empathic approach to self.

After a restless night's sleep, I have woken up feeling that something deep down has been stirred in me, if anything I am feeling a little agitated. My statement of the day is, 'Tell someone who gives a fuck'. That sums up how I feel, I can only reflect to my day yesterday. Firstly, a case discussion and then a discussion on Rogers 'Conditions of Worth', which is basically his theory that we as children are our true organismic self and that through the messages, we receive we become conditioned to thinking in a certain way and become distant from our organismic or real self. A simple example would be if you are told, 'If you do not pass your exams, you will be a failure throughout life,' you would then internalise this message and develop your adult with this message affecting your thoughts and actions. It became very evident from the experience in the room that we are walking around as adults still carrying those messages and that they still were affecting our lives. I have passed down messages I receive as a child to my own children not realising that they were wrong. Something I want to correct if I have not already.

During a very person-centred case discussion we were talking about a teenager who had multiple issues that he had come to counselling for. Everyone in the room expressed empathy and a real warmth towards this case. It was at that point that I wanted to shout out, "What about me? Where is the empathy for me and perhaps my teenager?" I never received that empathy at any point for anything I have ever been through; I just got on with it all. See, even now the voice in my head is saying, 'Stop playing the poor you, things were not that bad.' Do things have to be 'that bad' to receive empathy? No, of course not but it was at that moment that I realised the importance of genuine empathy and the effect it can have for the receiver. Throughout my day whether it is with clients or others in my life I can offer genuine empathy, I now realise how important that is. Sometimes I joke and say I have run out of empathy, and I guess sometimes that is true, I can feel drained and therefore unable to connect.

From now on I will be more empathic towards myself, it is all part of the be kinder to myself plan. I am going to acknowledge that I have had some tough times and that it is okay to offer myself some kind words. "That must have been really hard for you." With no judgment attached.

20 March, 2018

I talk about this protective bubble I have wrapped myself in, I can visualise it very clearly. Having dealt with extreme emotions for the past eight months I now find myself in a place of calm not an absence of feeling, a place where I will feel but experience it rather than reacting one way or another. Sure, I get upset but that upset is about feeling a little sorrow, empathic towards self and sad for the way other's act as I know it will affect them in the long run, at least that is my belief.

This realisation came about through an experience I had yesterday whilst at university. Our lecturer asked for someone to be his client and to sit in the middle of the room with him with all my fellow colleagues sitting around observing. This is something even as year ago I would have avoided, putting myself forward but for a change I put my needs first and took the therapy offered. The experience was a deep emotional experience, I sensed that he knew what was going on for me and made a connection with the sadness within. It was so intense that I forgot that I was sitting in the middle of a classroom with eleven other people watching, who also happened to be counsellors, I cried and released so much emotion at that point, leaving me emotionally drained until the next day. Afterwards everyone thanked me. 'What for?' I thought.

"For being brave," one group member said. "You always come across as so confident and strong; you were so brave to go through that in front of us all." Going on to say that she really admired me and had no idea I was going through so much, how I was doing it all. For me I knew that there was an opportunity to help myself and I took it. It was liberating to focus on what others would think, it was an experience to show the group, 'Yes, I am strong but also vulnerable and it is okay to be both.' It went on to trigger other emotional thoughts, there was a deep-rooted sadness I felt right in the pit of my stomach but when asked about the guilt I experienced it was cognitive I did not feel that in my body so informing me that it was a perception, learnt from others? I did not have an emotional connection with it, so time to let it go and address my inner sadness.

I am feeling what I have heard others refer to as 'spent', I am rather fond of that term. It sums me up rather well today. Emotionally, physically and cognitively spent! Time to get out of the routine, do something else, something restorative. Sure, I still have study and a mountain of other activities, but I will break the mundane and take time out of the spotlight. I give so much to everything I do; of course, I will be spent. The work is so important but so are the breaks otherwise you are no use to yourself or others.

The other realisations of the week are that, firstly I expect others to operate at the same level I do and secondly, I always want to see the best in people and encourage growth. The latter is easier to address, for as long as I can remember I have always been able to see the ability or potential in others. Especially when I was younger, I could accept the more negative points in favour of their potential as human beings. Having slightly moved away from that position I now find myself connecting with that position again. The difference this time, I will not let it be to my own growth or detriment. I never want to think that people are all bad, sounds naive but that is not my intention. I like to work with that little percentage of potential rather than condemning completely. Frustrating when the growth is not at the speed I would like or taken up, however a focal point for my work. I have also concluded if people act in negative way; they are only affecting their own future rather than affecting me, for I am responsible for my own destiny now.

That brings me to my first point I made about expecting others to operate on my level, the place I operate from. Feel bloody stupid now, what a crazy perspective to take. We all operate from our own place of being, that has been created from self, life and cognitive experiences. I now realise that my perception is just that, mine. We are all operating from different places that may be neither wrong nor right simply different. It has made me less judgmental, more accepting (well at least Monday to Friday!) I need to focus on my own place of being and growth area. Can you ever fully understand another's perspective, maybe not as there will be years of input into that one human? Sure, I am privileged to get to see a window but maybe never the whole self.

8 April, 2018

So very anxious and have been for over a week, want to withdraw from everyone so I do not have to keep up this pretence. That hollow feeling is back in the pit of my stomach again, not sure why? What is making me feel this way? Need just to be honest with everyone and say I feel empty, it is such a horrible feeling I just want it to go away.

Went away on an Easter break last week, normally would be family time. Somewhere deep down is a feeling of bereavement still such a change now, I need to give myself time to adjust to the new way. I want to just sit with it this time as busying me will not truly get to the bottom of the feeling. I am a bit annoyed as I have been doing so well, I did not want to go back, however it is telling me that it still needs dealing with. I had a day or two last week when I felt so empty, I did not care if I lived or died. What did it all matter anyway, I just wanted to disappear and that is what I am fighting today? Will anything ever make this better, I wonder, real uphill stuff. Now I know what I am missing from my life it has made it harder. I am still craving that one-to-one connection a relationship where I am safe to share my stuff as I have never truly felt this with any one. Yes, impatient, absolutely. I feel like I have been waiting my whole life for something I may never ever experience, complete tragedy. Never told any one my whole story and that seems so important right now, the whole thing beginning to the end. Spent a lonely Saturday night on my own, felt like a complete failure, I fucked up in life and that is what has led me to this point, for a split second wished I were oblivious to what I now know, want. Of course, I do not mean it, on a downer and want to sit here for a while. Want the whole world to fuck off and leave me alone, want to cry, feel sorry for myself and do not want to hear any words of fucking wisdom. Life is a fucking b*****d; it is hard work. Can you not see I am doing every fucking thing to change, move forward and it is hard, so hard? I am running out of answers for this shit. Help!

9 April, 2018

What drives me forward? It is an unknown force that I could never explain to make you understand, no disrespect to any of you, more a case of I just do not know. What I do know is that I need some stronger people around me to assist me on my travels, why? Because I do not always want to be the strong one it is tiring to say the least. Even if it were for a day, I would like to experience the feeling of someone watching over me taking care of me. I feel let down. Sure I do a good job of taking care of myself now, but I am a human being and have needs that are yet to be met. I do have a couple of friends now who see my bigger picture, and this is a huge comfort, people I do not have to explain myself to, they just get it. A real gift to me, going forward, I am still grateful for all I am provided with. My process is just busy right now and I am living in my head too much, can you be fed up thinking? Well, I am!

In conflict with what my needs are now. Having to deal with anything or any one is a struggle; however, the breaks are always hard as being busy at work means that I just get on with it all.

17 April, 2018

Craving lots of change now I have made the first move, want to talk to different people and get new perspectives; do not want to feel stuck ever again. I need to remember that if I am not satisfied then I must move on. Realised in general that I am living on hope, as when I look at this all I am basing my future on is a feeling or two. Knowing I do not want what is passing but still not clear on a future. Is that the way it must be, letting it all unfold bit by bit? I guess it does. Not seeing the value in planning as that could only lead to disappointment. I have loved every bit of it so far, even the sad desperate days have brought me a different perspective. Still feeling strong in my position but knowing that those around me are wondering what the hell I think I am doing. The family is worried about me, how could I possibly be coping with all this? I am getting used to dealing with things on my own and it feels good. I am buying my freedom; it will however come at a cost. The most scary, exhilarating thing I have ever done. If it all goes wrong, then I will only have myself to blame. The only real things that can now go wrong are my finances, putting a roof over our heads is really my only fear now. You see, I can cope with the other stuff. Money, the root of all evil? The thing we need to survive in this world, need enough to live, no ideas of grandeur. I really hope I can look back at this and say I made it; I got through that period of my life. You know what? I do not want to stop now, I want to keep going, pushing forward, achieving. What I always knew about myself.

Frustration is what it should be called – not divorce.

Who knew? It has made me regret ever being married (in an official sense) and ever wanting anything joint ever again. I am glad to writing this down as a record to remind me not to have joint anything again. I just want out, hate the bureaucracy of it all. Quite simple to marry but a bitch to reverse it. For a very emotional being I am being very methodical about the process, I have so far been able to deal with the divorce with no emotions attached; emotions are being kept somewhere else at present. Weird but I almost feel an absence of feeling, so much just does not affect me at present. How will I feel when it is all over? Is that the time the emotions will set in? Not sure. The only glimpse of emotion is hearing how you have wrecked someone else's life, dreams and plans. I am so sorry for that as my intention is never to hurt another, but there could be no other way out of this; I know it is what I must do. The train was leaving, and I wanted to leap on.

I feel truly blessed at this moment in time, like I have this base that is good and happy and full of hopes and dreams. No, not dreams as that makes the future seem unrealistic, just hopes. Sometimes I go away from the base to a place of fear, sadness, and anger but as much as I wonder, I come back to my warm happy place of complete uncertainty. Sure, I have questioned my mental health, would I know if I was going mad? Maybe not? But whether it is madness or hope I will keep walking forward. As I write this I laugh, this situation I find myself in is far away from what I had and I love the uncertainty, it is exhilarating.

4 April, 2018
Let go of the frustration, I am unable to make it go any

faster. Decided just to get on with my life and live for a while which as you know was always the plan this year, just to let my hair down and enjoy being. When I am in that mind frame everything seems manageable and okay. I am safe, happy and enjoying my mental freedom. Still so much to live for, I have released myself therefore in the process freed them too, opening my mind I am able to be more open minded for them too. I refuse to project into the future, after all my core belief is that, as I have said before, I will be okay and if it is meant to be it will happen, right? I am still sailing on those thoughts; you are your thoughts? Willing to give it a try.

New value has been put on everything in my life now. Appreciation for what I have in my life, not for what I have not. You cannot force life to come to you instead it will unfold and the reasons for events will unravel in front of you. If I were to jump forward too far then I would have missed other precious moments along the way, even the painful ones. So much no longer matters, I crave a simple life in many respects. I want to succeed in my own little way, I feel like I have succeeded. After all being a success should be a personal event not a global one. I am now who I truly want to be. I am living life by my own set of rules, and this will continue, a new happiness created by oneself, taken the power back. Such an exhilarating feeling. I trapped myself in other's core beliefs, restricted lives, so it would only be right that I set myself free and that is exactly what I am doing. Saying the word free I want to skip and dance and spin around, it fills me with much excitement, I had allowed words to oppress me now taking off that heavy load I am seeing and experience thoughts the eyes and mind of little me. These moments when I get these most magical feelings wash over me are priceless, it brings me to tears of such joy, priceless. Thank you.

Reading back over my own words I realise that it is like being in the ocean, riding the waves that represent my feelings crashing and banging, the very up and down emotions. I go under I come back up for air; I manage to keep my head above the water. Then the beautiful blue calm, the ebb and flow of life drawing me in and out.

I have now travelled so far, I am unable to get back home, and there are tears, a huge sadness for what has passed, for just a while I feel as if I am on a runaway train, and I cannot get back. I ask myself back where? Back to my old life? My family unit the way it was? I am not quite sure just feelings of this new life moving on so far that I could not possibly go back even if I wanted to. A year on and I am starting to miss the essence of my marriage, not the entirety of it but those comfortable moments you share with another. I am not lost, maybe on unfamiliar ground that is making me only what I can describe as home sick. The comforts of my old life vanished.

Comfortable, is where I am now. I have come to a place of acceptance to where I am, enjoying what I have and being at peace with who I am. I do not fit into people's boxes, and hopefully never will. I like free thinking people, those who do not try to make you fit anywhere, sure we all judge however I like to work with what is in front of me.

I have also found my voice, no longer going to be a bystander. I have lots of informed opinions to share with the world and I am not afraid to do so. A whole new inner confidence that I have created for me, by me. I want to meet and talk to new people and share thoughts and feelings. That said, I have this ridiculously small voice waiting for something to go wrong. "Enjoy what you have, as it won't last." Trying to look round the corner to see what is going to happen. Of course, I know that is impossible, does not stop me doing it though.

1st May, 2018

So, what now? This question popped into my head yesterday. I have spent almost a year working on the product that is me. I have my mojo back, my thirst for living and I wake up most days in my happy place. As I look back over the year it has been hard on a very personal level, thankful for all that has been provided for me. My friends who have had to listen to me going over and over this stuff and my inspirational girls whom you are fully aware I burst with pride at the sheer mention of their names. Still, lots of change ahead but it is all feeling rather positive. It is almost like I feel ready for something but am not sure what that thing is. I do not want to stop now or ever.

Whilst in a CBT lecture yesterday and the tutor formulating a client for me, I realised the formulation related to my own life and that my safety behaviour was my marriage, I had this negative inner voice making me believe I could not cope on my own. In true CBT style I dropped the safety behaviour (my marriage) and hey presto I now know I can. I have been doing the graded hierarchy on myself and it works, raising my anxiety through anxiety producing situations, however stupidly I went for the highest first. Realise now better to start with the small stuff work up the ladder not down!

What do I do with this excess energy I have? The feeling I have is of excitement, life's potential just became huge. Want to do new things, have new experiences, talk to as many people as possible. Feeling a bit hyperactive. Maybe this new energy for life has been provided so I can tackle the next chapter, the next bit of the big D, my move, finishing my course? Forgot to mention still have lots going on but now not fazed by any of it, that feeling I talk about, "It will all be okay." I want to spread the word. Go on and jump, the feeling at the end is amazing, cannot remember feeling like this. Want to run around spreading my positivity. I believe in myself for the first time ever, this girl certainly can. I want a life that is full.

2nd May, 2018
There are days like today when I miss being loved, being held by someone and for me to know it will all be okay. Of course, I do know that, however being held by someone else and hearing those words is comforting. No matter how good I feel or how happy I am, I am a human being with needs, and love is so important in my everyday life. Waking up this morning I wanted the comfort you get from a relationship, the unspoken, and the contact. I drive home from work wanting to share my day with someone who will listen, someone who wants to hear about my day. My eldest and I talk many times during the day, and she really does listen to me, I run things by her, and she understands. She is a real-life line to me. I do not want to get to depend on her, do not get me wrong we have a two-way dialogue that I absolutely love. These things are not necessary a need but now a want. I have realised I am not needy of much, but have a clear

idea of what I want, two vastly different things. It has taken me a while to work out what the difference was and how better it is for me to want these aspects rather than needing them. Let me explain I feel very self-sufficient now, I can provide myself with lots of things and can now make myself happy. Standing in this position gives me the space to think about what I want now. Surprisingly, it is the little thing I want, and I have to say communication is at the top of my list. Having someone who can actively listen to what I say and have a deep understanding of who I am. This basic counselling skill is so important in forming a relationship, being heard, genuine empathy and an understanding. I guess all the things I provide for others I now want back in return as I realise their worth. What I want from life seems quite simple, Health for me and my girls, interesting worthwhile work, a roof over my head, to live instead of just existing and a fulfilling relationship. Simple!

I am no longer unhappy, so my thoughts are noticeably clear and focused now. I do not want what I thought I needed at the beginning of this process; I am in a quite different place. I am also beginning to love myself for who I am faults and all; nothing is any longer so bad that it will hold me back from living, my life my choices, my inner peace.

Life taught me to be private, not to share your thoughts feelings, and keep it all in. I am now busting at the seams; all I want to do is talk. I want to talk to people about my life about how I am feeling. Yes, it is time to talk! Such an alien feeling for me, I have tried and tested talking and it has not had a detrimental outcome. I have nothing to hide, don't get me wrong I still have boundaries, such a therapist thing!

Just that I can express myself to those in my life now. Sharing experiences can be helpful not only to ourselves but also to those around us. I guess part of what held me back was being judged, but we all judge, I just hope people see me for who I am not what I am, I am not going to hide that anymore. You will get judged anyway so why not make it easier and say this is who I am. Now thinking that I am becoming very liberal through these experiences of the last year or maybe going back to being liberal, I am just in the head space of I understand. Life is not straight forward, the road ahead will twist and turn, I guess I was trying to go forward in a straight line and did not allow for what the road looked like. Also, there will be stops and starts, endings, new beginnings, even experiences that I did not plan but that is all okay.

"Think big," was said to me yesterday, it keeps repeating in my head. A massive fear of mine, I have kept everything small and manageable. Why? Because I did not want to be seen to fail, by myself or those around me. I have taken away my safety blankets and I am feeling exposed, wondering what I can achieve. I have one foot in the yes, I can achieve big things and the other hoovering over keep it small. I wonder what my future is going to hold now, have I changed my path? Part of me would love to have a peep; the other half just wants it to unfold gradually.

My whole view of the world and self has changed, and it has freed me in a way I could never have imagined. I have unlocked the padlock and I am now travelling free, almost feel liberated. I am in that driving seat, no more should or fixed ideas. I have even got fiercely protective of my space and time, okay for friends to be around but I am finding enjoyment I never knew existed. Still a small fear of all this newfound life to come to a halt and going back to flat lining, still must just enjoy what I have while I have got it.

Endings, had quite a few of them recently and have been grieving, however have come to a place of being at peace with endings, maybe because I have experienced first-hand that unless you close that door behind you the other will not open. When seeing clients, I always disliked endings, would have always rather skipped that last session, avoided the awkward thanks and goodbye. Why? Maybe I had never experienced a positive ending or realised that most of life is temporary. About eighty percent there with that concept. It has freed me to live, yes just to live, as with the forever thing I was always cautious George, what ifs galore. No point in doing that if it is going to end, absolute crazy. That way I was not experiencing new things as let us face it not so much long-term stuff around. Seems so obvious now, bet you are reading this thinking, 'Is she for real?'

Knowing things and experiencing them are quite different. Thoughts of turning into a walking platitude, which does humour me somewhat, all those positive messages you receive through social media that I have connected with throughout this journey are now some days fucking annoying. Missing my negative shit, cannot help it but let us face it, not quite realistic if you are positive every day. Sure, have coping strategies but nothing like my old friend negativity showing its face just for a few moments. Realisation that I hold on to things just in case, have heard that from clients over and over. After all society sends a message that one is lonely, but it does not have to be, so glad I have had this experience, never been on my own. Being on one's own is quite different to being lonely and I am so extremely fortunate never to have been lonely, it must be a horrible place to be. I have a choice to put myself forward and to communicate with others; the whole process is two ways.

Whilst walking down my high street on Saturday I had a chance meeting with a tutor from my counselling training. She stopped me to say hi, we talked about what we were doing now. She, newly retired, asked how my work was going so I explained all I was doing and followed it up with how fortunate I was (not a believer in luck). She replied with I hear it is very tough out there to which I agreed. She then commented that from what she knew of me I always put myself out there and therefore implying that I had created what was going on for me work wise. I walked away feeling positive as I was not aware that others had recognised my effort in making all this work. I have and continue to work hard to get to wherever it is I am going, fortunate defiantly as I love my work, it is not a job it is part of who I am, what I stand for in life and the very essence of self. Worth every bit of the continued effort.

20 May, 2018

Very reflective weekend as going to a school reunion, it has been almost thirty years since I had walked through those gates. The places had changed so much in that time, I hardly recognised the place. So many people I did not remember or had forgotten about. The people I sat with were those who knew me from the age of eleven, we all sat laughing, the connection still there and we laughed and made fun of one another. They were uncomplicated, I could be myself and feel relaxed no need to explain. Almost picking up from where we left off from.

My teenage years were chaotic, not sure why but it all just spiralled out of control, would going back be part of the repair I wondered. I have a sense that I have been trying to recover from it all since, the sweeping it all under the carpet had not worked, can I finally put it all behind me now? I had judged myself so harshly over the years and had expected others to do the same. I now show the teenagers I work with kindness and understanding of their situations and relationships, a respect for what they are experiencing. So, you have messed up, does not have to define the rest of your life. That message is for both them and me I expect.

Going back has proved one thing, my life has moved on so much. I have achieved more than the expectations of that school. We all decided that we had not received an education that we could be proud of in fact hardly anyone remembered learning very much. What was evident was that we all went through life back then and it would have been good to have had people we could have talked to.

End of term numbness is what I will now refer to this feeling as. Recognising that it occurs the week before every end of term or half term. The tears, the sadness, tiredness and absence of real feeling. It is getting easier to deal with as I have now recognised that I am okay. Just in need of some me time, reflection and processing time. Go to my cut of point of not being able to hear any more, my cup is overflowing. Time to put some things for myself in place. I promised myself that I would take better care of myself as the scales had started to go in others favour leaving me saying, "What about my feelings?" I have let it slip again, but awfully hard to keep that balance when your job is a giving job. I put so much of my heart and soul into what I do, it is part of who I am. I do recognise it is a constant juggling act. Will I ever achieve the balance? I could be happy in a dark room with my thoughts for a couple of days, just enough time to recover. Before it then all starts again...

I look out of my bedroom window; how will I really feel on the day I have to leave my home? I want to move on but that does not mean that there will not be more grieving. Worried about my children for it is their family home, the place you retreat to. I so wanted to create that somewhere else for them, I realise it can never be the same, but I hope we can make new memories together. Another thing to go through, not sure what it will look like, hoping not to fall flat on my face. I have got to get this right, now all my responsibility. Even though I do not want to continue to live in this space, I am of course saddened as I have lived in that house for just over eighteen years now. However, I do want my own space now, I still feel that whilst I am still living here, I cannot mentally move forward as it is constantly in the back of my head that it is fast approaching.

The thought has passed through that will I ever feel settled ever again? Looking back over the past year I went through an unsettled period where I was a little mentally unstable, I certainly feel more balanced and grounded now. I can only describe it as being let out and feeling free, a feeling that has subsided now. At present I crave time on my own.

The question for me is what got me to this point; this is where I will start to struggle as now, I must bring others into my picture. More than happy to talk about me now but reflecting and looking historically makes me anxious. Look I am not setting out here to incriminate any one, play the blame game again once more or judge. Really just want you to know in my eyes what got me to fuck it.

So, council estate kid from big working-class family manages to get pregnant at eighteen, stop the press. Judged, I sure was by all around me and even those who did not know me. Regressing slightly in my early childhood I wanted to dance, play the piano and from what my mum has told me grow up to drink champagne and drive a red Ferrari. Fucked that little one up, or have I? Anyway, so here I am – eighteen with a single parent with a baby, a little flower so very pretty and perfect in every way. So, it begun, living at home with everyone giving their opinion and feeling like I was living in a pressure cooker. Look, do not get me wrong. I will be eternally grateful for being given a secure base and support but maybe never the autonomy I craved must have put them all under pressure too, for that I am sorry. What do you do now? In my eyes I have two options: become a statistic and fall into the social norm or work my way out of my little situation.

Within six months I was in central London training to become a Fitness professional, the best five hundred pounds I have ever spent. From then onward juggling motherhood with the help from my family and a very thriving career. Thinking about it my pattern ever since has been to literally work hard and move myself forward, never shy of hard work. I did my best, not the greatest mum that has ever been, but I did my best with the skills I had at the time. That little flower grew up to also be a hard worker and more than that a courageous woman who is very capable of making life happen, she is funny and clever and loved beyond words.

We all come from systems, units of people doing there best with there own life experiences and baggage to carry around. Every family has its good parts and challenging edges , mine no different, another experience I have learnt allot from, I hold my truth and do not need others to agree or disagree anymore. No child is parented by the same parent, each relationship within that system is complex and evokes different feelings.

Life told me just to keep walking and to work hard, the culture of talking about mental health was just not apart of my world growing up as I am sure it was not for many. I guess life did not allow what I now believe is a luxury, that being the time and space to talk and to develop in life. I am truly grateful that I have been able to gift myself that time, which of course then enhances the unit I have created, it goes on and on.

Research shows us that if long term stress and anger is not dealt with it raises the cortisol levels in the body causing illness. Those who express their feeling are known to live longer (Sue Gerhardt, Why Love Matters). Sorry but you are all going to now know exactly how I feel as I want to keep on living for quite some time. I will embrace the holistic approach to my everyday being.

If you sat all the five siblings down, we would all tell you a quite different story as to what our childhood was like. Individually we are all quite different, I guess I never quite fit in as I had vastly different ideas that I soon learnt to squash. I must admit I am unconventional in many ways, or I was and now intend on being again. Maybe that alone has been the hardest single thing I have had to do, step away but if I do not, I will continue to plateau with no forward movement. I love them all dearly and hope one day things may be different. Misunderstood is how I have felt most of my life, I guess I have never understood myself so how could other possibly. There is no one person out there that I have been able to share all of me with.

I went on to have one more daughter ten years after my first little flower. My second daughter just as wonderful as the first, vastly different but strong and in my eyes an amazing human being. All this has been hard on both my girls in very different ways. They do not have my vision and sure everything they know is changing but I want to reassure them that I will always be available to them and that everything will be all right, and it will.

Mother-daughter relationships are far more complicated than I could ever imagine. Until I stepped away from my mum I never really reflected on its complexities. History does seem to repeat itself as much as you try to do something different. I am desperately trying to fix this all. Time to finally repair…

I have very different relationships with both of my girls, why? It is simple really, I love them equally however they are different people therefore evoking different feelings in me, and secondly as mum I have been ever evolving and have changed and will hopefully keep changing, so it is impossible not to be different with them both. The truth is that I tried my best with the resources I had at the time and will continue to try my best with the resources I have going forward. But they will both be loved eternally. They have got me through the dark days without even knowing it.

8 August, 2018

You know when you are happy as you can just sit by yourself doing nothing and feel the same, well that is my hypothesis anyway. Last summer I would have been unable just to be, I was in too much pain. I have found a new inner happiness that I am proud to say I created by myself, never knew this feeling existed or rather it was possible to be created on my own. Realisation today that I can only cope with me still now, not sure when or if that will change but I need to be in my own company. Sure, I love meeting my friends and going out, interacting with others through my work and life itself but happy to come back to my safe peaceful space. No longer wanted to share that space, well not presently anyway. That is a big shift as I spent the first eight months repeating that I did not want to be on my own, well now I am comfortable to be as one.

So, what do you do with a newfound happiness? Weird question I know, but it feels as if I have this thing and I want to do something with it but am not sure what. I guess I am on the road to being okay and looking for my next challenge. I took on the world this year and survived, so what is next? Realisation! I am still sitting in the void that is the divorce, waiting. Still pushing forward only to hit resistance. The way I have learnt to cope with it is to detach myself from it all. Let me explain. So I have me, my soon to be ex-husband, my children and the divorce. Obviously, I am referring to the components involved in my divorce. Oh yes and the expense, who knew it was so expensive? Anyway, my rationale for it all so far and of course this could change. I am working on me, investing in my work and enjoying my newfound happiness, still in my bubble.

Then there is of course the divorce, frustrating and slow and to a certain amount out of my control. This could have been so simple; I just want out to start the next phase, along this road. So, to cope with it I have taken my feelings out of the procedure, this is now a business transition. I will and do deal with my feelings elsewhere. I guess that is true in all this now. I have learnt finally to separate emotions from the practicalities of life in general. The expense is a little worrying but I so far, I am managing so until I can't keep going. If we over thought most things, we would not do anything. I am not afraid to live now, that feels amazing to be able to say.

4th September, 2018

Nothing is moving at the pace I would like, still stuck in the vault that is my divorce. Trying so hard not to fall in the trap of turning into the divorce monster. That being bitter, angry and very twisted. Easier said than done, I have had days where I could be truly angry at the system and him for playing around with my future life. You see I am still of the belief that I cannot move on until I leave the family home. Of course, financially I am better off where I am for the time being and I know I have this huge mountain to climb in moving, physically, financially and mentally. Scared, sure I am, I have never done this before and if I think about it too long, I go into a bit of override. I want to get it over with now; the anticipation is making me tense. Although there is still an underlining excitement for what is to come, not that I have a clue what that even looks like. That vision of me shutting my front door, standing behind it and knowing that it is my own peaceful place is enough. My needs are small in life now; when it comes down to it your inner happiness is what matters, whatever that may look like for you.

Treading water? That is how it feels now. The next push will not happen until I can go through the final part of this, and that is out of my control. So, what do I do now? Even though mentally exhausted at times I keep pushing forward. One day leads to another and another and a step further forward. It will have to come to an end at some point is what I tell myself.

Had a mini meltdown yesterday then felt guilty as I am so fortunate and so much to be grateful for. I was angry, fed up being the one to cope, the one that does not moan about anything, I wanted to lie down and not get up. Take some time off and have a break down, go off the rails. Here I am, Tuesday morning, back at work on time with plans to go to the gym later. Rock and fucking roll!

I am okay, I keep telling myself. Which of course I am and in a completely different place to the one I was last year. Still running with the theory that it has been okay so far there is no indication to the contrary. Of course, I have just made my life much harder as starting again at my age is never going to be easy. However, that cannot make me turn back now or ever.

Still trying to enjoy this interim period as much as possible.

What price does freedom come at?

11 September, 2018

Freedom is something I want now but it is going to come at a cost. This is something that I did obviously not consider when getting married. I am finding the legality of getting out of this tough. I took the blame even though all I was guilty of was falling out of love. Now he has been allowed to drag his heels over absolutely nothing and almost control my destiny. The only way out is to go to court which brings me to my point at what price does freedom come? I now must find a rather large sum of money to ask the judge to force this whole situation along. How can this be fair? I can tell you it is not. My rather simplistic way forward would to be a time limited system where both parties legally must engage with a set fee. This is putting my already limited funds at some strain and my ongoing plans for somewhere to live under a big question mark. Of course, I will continue as I am determined to have the end prize, independence and freedom. No way am I going to let this break me, but it will be at a cost.

September 13th, 2018

Woke up today after a great night's sleep with the thought that I am no longer looking to change who I am. Narcissistic tendencies, no this is something different I promise you. For my whole life I have tried to fit in to other boxes of the way I should be, I will no more do this. Sure, my behaviour is challengeable sometimes and that is a working progress. However, this is me now, take me or leave me. For the first time I am happy and confident with who I am, not afraid to reveal myself now. What was I so afraid of, someone not liking me? I am sure I am not everyone's cup of tea but that is okay too.

Questioning phase has started now, how I really felt about my relationships, what did I ignore and for what reason. Some things were just never right but I guess I thought that was natural and I had to just get on with it all. I realise now that I have found an inner peace and happiness that I do not have to settle ever again for anything that is not quite right. No longer having to put up and shut up. I am lucky to have choice and I am thankful for that. In fact, I have lots to be thankful for, over the last fourteen months I looked outwards for some happiness, realising now I had all I needed right in front of me. Myself, my amazing girls and a great array of friends. Plus, a career I love. Anything else now will be a bonus.

19 September, 2018

In such a different place to even the one I was back in the spring. I can only describe it like being in some sort of recovery and getting stronger every day. All my initial thoughts have disappeared. As annoying as I am going to find this, I had no idea what I wanted initially, could have run myself into the completely wrong situation. It has taken a massive amount of strength to sit tight and hold on to what I believed I could create. Still holding on to that and continuing I must take other perspectives in to do the best I can do for us. I am learning the art of patience; I simply cannot have what I want when I want it. It sometimes takes a little longer.

I have also had to own up to my faults; sometimes I do want it all my own way and have been very unreasonable. I need to keep this in the balance going forward.

Scared now of what new relationships look like at this stage. What are the expectations, not in any rush as I really like my life on my own? Guess I have that new chapter all to come.

1st October 2018

Finding out what it is I like, what I want from life is harder than I may have imagined. I want to talk to someone, so I could share my inner thoughts but don't have that person. You see it would have to be someone who was emotionally intelligent, not too many of those people around me now. More to the point does someone really want to sit listening to all I have to say, all I am thinking feeling. Probably not, especially as my thoughts are fast moving. I currently have an overactive process going on. I could go into counselling but not even ready for that yet either. Strange words for a therapist, but I have the belief you need to be ready for therapy, and I am not quite there yet.

Can I go it alone? Yes and no. No because I am not from a lone background. You see, I grew up in a household with six others; this does not best prepare you for solitude. In fact, far from it. It is not that I do not like being on my own, it is just an alien concept. What I am trying to work out is do I want to be on my own or is happiness being with others. Recently I have had a lot of pleasure spending time with old friends and new acquaintances, hearing different perspectives, other voices. Having never lived on my own or thought of doing this at this stage, it has sent me into a bit of a spin.

2nd October, 2018

Woke up this morning feeling a little scared that I will not be able to provide a stable home for my daughter and myself. I can't fail her or myself, I have always been able to climb that mountain and keep going. This morning I would just like to give up, the fight forward it too hard. Realisation that I will be my only resource, guess I always have been, but the financial situation is weighing me down a little. Not worried about much just keeping a roof over our heads, living in a bubble now, a happy bubble most of the time, do I need to step out of it yet? My instinct is telling me just to take a step back and enjoy what is in front of me now. Worrying never helped any one, standing here on this Monday I really do not have any one thing to worry about. My checklist is we are safe, we have a roof over our heads and support for what we are going through now. My worries are all in the future that may never be. Mindfulness needs to be practiced, live in the moment, notice what is going on around you try not to live in the past or the future.

8 October, 2018

Week two of feeling low, I was doing so well. Just emotionally drained I guess, and I am finding it hard to pull myself out of it all. Classic feelings of not wanting to get out of bed, overwhelmed with everything, not feeling like I can cope and no real desire to do anything or be anywhere.

Trying my best to live in the day but that has become difficult. Must face the court proceedings now, which is so daunting, I am clear on what I am doing but cannot quite believe it has come to this. I must accept I did all I could and tried to prevent this from happening.

Telling those around me bits of what is going on, but no one knows the full extent of my down mood now. I am worryingly down; I will tell my supervisor next week. I am just fed up saying to people about this all, exhausting.

How grateful I was today when that little voice said,

"Love you to the moon and back." My heart once again melted. Love in a pure form.

Just cannot shift this down feeling – anxious, I would even gone so far as a little unstable. Not sure how I am managing to keep going, but work is my place of sanctuary, there is nowhere to hide so I plough through my day. Again, finding it hard being without a companion, a weird one as can function fine. Take Sunday for instance, would have liked to spent a Sunday with someone just talking and relaxing. How nice would it be having someone else to take care of me for a change? That is hard, having to be your own everything. Right now, I need everything to stop and for me to get off for a while. My job leaves nowhere to hide.

Is this now my future? Is my true happy place out there, I am running out of steam for all of this. Mentally broken, shattered in many places, the more I go down the more the shit keeps coming up. I do not like myself, feel horrible, feel like becoming a recluse never getting out of bed ever again. Is this worse than fifteen months ago, I guess simply different this is about me on a very personal note. Not sure how much longer I can meet everyone's demands on me.

9 October, 2018

Not sure how much of how I feel are real feelings and how much is from outside expectations. Let me explain, deep down I am okay, not anywhere near to where I need to be and who knows how long that will take or what it will bring. Frustrated, as I am in a holding bay, although I have the funny feeling that it is going to be yet another uphill struggle. Have now to go through lots to get to the next chapter in my life, whatever that may be. Getting through each day by trying to live moment to moment interacting with the world around me, work and supporting my family in an increasingly changing way.

I know I am not ready for the next chapter as lots of stuff to sort out in the middle, that including myself. Although I know my own mind very well, quite sure about what I don't want and open to new life experiences, happy to go alone if I can have some company along the way, don't want to be on my own forever. I crave that connection with another person, but this time I want the emotional connection so I can tell them almost everything and for them to understand me. Happy to live my own life alongside that, just be nice to have that someone out there for me. That triggers a reoccurring thought that I want things in a selfless way for me now. I do not want things experiences to be shared, just want people out there for me, Sara, I have done being there for everyone else, done that period of my life. Always been there for everyone else's needs, in my private life and my work. Yes, I am to blame for part of that as I let it go on. Maybe I did not know how to stop it. However, I do now. I want my own private life the part that is just for me. Experiences I do not have to share with others unless I choose too.

14 October, 2018

So, it seems that I have been skirting around what it is I have needed to do. Everything is out of control. I am changing all aspects of my life and it is an uphill struggle. I have decided to say the D word and it has made me feel like rubbish. I know it is what I must do but now the grieving process starts, avoidance with a capital A. I feel like I have been run over by a bus. This is the only thing that will make everything else eventually fall into place, but in the meantime, I have got to go through the painful part of this journey, and I must sit with this for a while, again frustration but the only way I can move forward. How did I think that I could sit in this holding bay for two years? That would be two more years towards fifty and two more wasted years. No, I need to act now, I just want someone to come along and scoop me up and tell me everything is going to be okay. That is just not going to happen; I must climb this steep hill on my own with the support of the people around me. I am back to that knot in my stomach.

16 October, 2018

Feelings coming and going, as low-level anxiety still lies at the pit of my stomach. I guess that I feel different after saying what I wanted; knowing that I must implement it is another thing. There will be no one that understands this fully, but I am sure this is what I want to do need to do.

So, the hardest part is now approaching, I need to find some inner strength and faith from somewhere. Tagged along with the belief that this will get better, accepting that I am in a lonely place and that it is not as scary as I was telling myself it was helping me. I am resourceful and self-motivated so therefore have the capacity to be self-sufficient. After all we really can only rely on ourselves. Yes, we can take the support of others but no one as reliable as self. As soon as we accept that, things start to look better. That alongside a sense of humour, mine keeps me going most days, laughing at myself and the world around me has defiantly kept me going.

17 October, 2018

Feeling positive again today, I guess facing the tough parts of this are hard, but you have to go through them to get to whatever else is ahead. Basically, not productive to use the avoidance tactic.

Feeling a little stronger to push forward with this on my own, I can do this. It is just a strange concept, only having you to rely on. Not being able to turn around to the person you have always gone to but instead relying on your own judgement. Empowering, I like it, I want this freedom, independence. Sure, there is a tough road ahead, realising that this all comes down to money, a reason others do not go it alone.

Everything is still out of control, but I guess that is what transition brings. You are neither at the start or the end of this road.

30 October, 2018

Every day a new emotional state. Last week was full of anxiety, that empty feeling at the pit of my stomach, not even able to attach the feeling to anything apart from the future. Yes, the future trying so hard not to project into the future but finding it hard not to want to have a peep. How can I possibly know what is out there for me? Everything is changing daily and that includes my feelings. Not sure what I want in the next hour let alone the next year.

In tears again today, just want to get it all out but that is not always possible with everyone around. I hear what you are thinking; again, hear she goes trying to keep a brave face on it all. I am not; just do not want any one having answers for my feelings. There are none. I am just sitting in this shit, working through it, waiting for the whole lot to pass.

Everyone saying how brave I am, how strong I am. Yes, I am those things but also vulnerable, sometimes I just want to be scooped up and held tightly by someone telling me this whole thing will be okay. Guess what? That is not going to happen, the saying is that you can only make yourself happy, no one can do it for you, guess there is a lot of truth in that but others around you do impact on your happiness. Or rather we let them impact on us. I am definitely starting to look inward for the answers, even making myself laugh at some of my internal tragedy. Wow, how self-centred I have begun to be. Trying not to do the poor me thing, but I guess I feel a little sorry for myself today and I am trying to self soothe like a toddler would with a favourite toy. I have decided it is okay to feel sorry for you if it does not last for too long as wallowing long term is not a good look. That is my problem you see (one of) everyone sees me as strong and getting on with it all. Maybe I do not show my vulnerable side enough.

Life has caught up with me, all the stuff I just got on with and coped with has taken its toll, and it is all right to say it out loud. I stood still and like dominos everything fell behind me, with me still standing upright. This is not going to take me down; sure, it will rock me and make me wobble, but I am still standing in the only way I know how to. I have never given myself the time to deal with anything. Always just brushed me down and charged ahead.

My expectations of people are way too high. I ask for honesty (filtered at times) and compassion for others around, and understanding of who we are and why?

Kindness, emotional intelligence, acceptance and loyalty, what about what we want from ourselves, again back to looking inward, needing to get what we need from ourselves. What can I provide from me?

No one thing could fix this, I guess it has taken a long time to build this life, like a coil spinning around and around, now a long time to unwind it all. I am doing all I can, exercise, talking to others, socialising, working, doing things I enjoy. All the Cognitive Behavioural Therapy you could eat! But still, I must wait for the bereft feeling to pass. I guess that is what I am dealing with here, I am bereft, and things are passing, with me still trying to function. To a certain degree I am doing okay, not quite gone under yet!

7 November, 2018

Will this period ever end?

Anxiety, low mood, are two things I am going through currently, it is a daily battle as those feelings are not good. Sheer determination and more CBT to get me out of the door each day. This period is difficult; I do not want to feel this way. This is not about me turning back as there is no doubt in my mind, I made the right move but being stuck is hard going. Maybe I have avoided how I refer to 'sitting in the shit' of course you cannot avoid it if you are to truly to move forward, I was stupid as I am guessing if I had not avoided this I would have moved past this stage. My little friend hindsight saying hello again.

Trying to practice getting through one day at a time. What is wrong with me now? I am unable to work it out, all I know is I hope is not my destination. Guessing that is my fear, I have gone through this, and I will end up having a shit unhappy life. I must continue to believe in what I can create; negativity is dragging me down. I am aggravating myself.

Quotes of the day.

If plan A did not work the alphabet has 25 more letters. Just because my path is different does not mean I am lost.

The one who falls and gets up is so much stronger than the one who never fell.

Difficult roads often lead to beautiful destinations. (Bloody hope so)

How important my sense of humour has become!

"City of dreams"

I have so much more to give and receive, please do not let this be it!

9 November, 2018

Decided to enter the world of social media. My privacy is important, but I need to remember that I am in control of it and not the other way around. Previously thought it was just an invasion of privacy and I was a little frightened of it all. The pressure of having to post and take interesting pictures are another annoyance. Looking at it in a different way now, stopping the isolation, it is good to have some contact with the outside world and I guess people that are not in my everyday life. Already had a laugh with my old school friend who decided it would be amusing to post a picture of us looking rather amusing. Let us face it (pardon the pun). It is now their number one way to communicate as much as I am still against it. I am not virtual, as my youngest said,

"Mum, think you are better in real life." This is true. Human contact is always going to be my preference, but in an increasingly busy world a little banter and connection might just get me out of my own head for a while. Brings me back to nothing is forever, if it works for you at the time then go for it.

Level is just how I am feeling this week, which is great, would even go as far as glimmers of happiness. What a difference from the past couple of weeks, and the reason? Who knows? It is true, feelings do come in waves, obviously not for no reason but mostly without warning. More about how strong I am feeling to cope with the waves, also going with the feelings instead of trying to bat them away. I know I am feeling better this week as I have not been to the gym or been walking around with my headphones in, avoidance I had realised is what I was doing!

It is now practicing what I have preached for so long, human contact. With the right human contact, we can grow and develop, and life is so much more fun with some others around us. I can do solitude, which is all important in life, but we can cope better as we can also switch to self-reliance from time to time.

Feeling numb now, almost like I know everything is going on, but I have removed myself just outside of the picture for a while. Is this a coping strategy? Almost like an out-of-body experience. I am watching my life with the feeling of being partly removed. Another new feeling to start the week.

I must take good care of myself now as I have even more people taking from me, to be able to continue I need to look after myself like I have never done before. Even, dare I say it out loud, put myself first sometimes? Scary concept. I need everyone out of my space at times, just so I can think. Still with the belief I have so much more to give in this life, I could almost cry, please let me show the world what I can offer? Wow, that fills me with extreme excitement. I need to get out there and be ready for what is now unfolding. Change has already started for me. I feel fortunate. Thank you, world.

1st January, 2019

What will the start of the New Year bring me? Finally, an end to the divorce proceeding. It will have to as my youngest will go to university if all goes to plan for her and I now have a court date. I tried to block it thinking that he would come to his senses, always the optimist but unfortunately not. It has been said that I always like to see the good in people, this is partly true. I guess when I feel someone has potential as a human being, I will always want to encourage that. Anyway, most of the time when people do you wrong, it comes back on them not you, if you do not let them sway you off your path.

I created a new path for myself and have a new inner strength and calmness created though going through the toughest time of my life, of which I had tried to avoid from time to time. Or maybe the path was always there I just got a bit lost. Literally sitting in the shit worked. I remind myself that I got through the last nineteen months I can get through all day by day. I have documented this before and I am still not sure of the reason, but I worry a lot less now. Nothing seems to phase me; maybe I have better coping strategies? Whatever it is I feel I will get to a solution or at least there is one out there.

Christmas was very different, that is the bit that must be accepted to move on and not feel so terrible. New traditions are made or the flexibility to change is now present. It will never be the same, or have the same meaning but that is okay, I would not want it to be the same. I am so fortunate; I have this newfound support network behind me if I allow it.

January, 2019
I can no longer sell my soul.

2nd February, 2019
Procrastinating – need to move forward and deal with the court case, it is not going away. As much as I would have liked it to. I asked for help, as I need someone to sit down with me and hold my hand and to make sure I am getting on with this now. I do not want to go to court of course, bury my head and wake up when it is all over. I am a little scared, tinged with my overall feeling that this will be okay, well I must believe that as otherwise what would be the point? I am once again stuck, the next part of this unable to move forward until the court decides my fate.

Sadness has washed over me again; the divorce is going ahead, documents lodged at court the exchange went ahead. No idea that it would leave me so emotional. I am not fit for work, so I take time out, the first time I have allowed myself through all of this. Not available for any one work-wise so I practice what I peach and take some mental health days off. Just what I wanted to avoid all this happening at once, having to keep this all in at home as A-Levels are approaching so I am spending my days off back on the school run, cooking and nurturing my baby who is about to leave me. I am really having to go this next part alone and I am scared once again of fucking it all up. A fuck up – that is just how I feel. How much longer will this go on? Please release me from all this now.

18 June, 2019

After the court date, I realised a couple of things, firstly there really is no fairness in life, no one to hear your voice and the law is defiantly a complete arse. Why do we continue with this antiquated system that offers nothing unless you have an endless pot of money somewhere? I want to stand up for all the people out there that do not have a voice and have been at the mercy of the court system that is simply not fit for practice. I have tried not to be angry after all I have been told that, "It was you that wanted this." Yes, I made a choice that I wanted to turn left instead of right, I have not killed anyone or committed a crime but just wanted something else other than to be married. This is 2019, surely I should be able to have a voice and be able to move on. There needs to be a new system in place that allows you to make that decision without having to be at the mercy of another's games for as long as they please and at your cost.

18 June, 2019

Riding the waves of my emotions, those days when I feel low are familiar now and I am finding them more manageable? They do not last forever, after all everything passes. Still living in frustration, I try to divert my attention as much as possible, re focusing myself and trying hard every day to be positive yet kind to me. Mostly I can know what is best for me and able to make decisions that will go along with my ever-changing emotions. In contrast okay to have the low days as they are important as well.

Feelings are so important now, after all this decision was all made on a feeling, the same feeling that drives me forward. It is not based in cognition; not really having a plan, just pushing forwards with what feels right. Reckless? It certainly does not feel like that, the feeling that this is right for me and that I need to keep driving on lives in me.

I now have a feeling that I need to surround myself with likeminded, open-minded people. Not of the same opinion just those who are open to change is becoming important. The whole law of attraction theory is a constant in my thoughts right now. Sending out positive messages to draw what and who I need right now. I need to get out into the world and see what else I need to find, try new things.

October, 2019

I was once told, "Believe in what you can create," well I did and through some very tough personal days things finally seem to be moving forward in a way I could never believe. I am scared that this is suddenly going to all fall as I never believed I could get anywhere near to my dream. In no way do I believe that this is near the end, just the beginning of many more happy days. I hope it has all been worth it as there have been many days I wanted to just give up as I was walking this path blindly. All so far has been led with how I felt about things, no logic or even reason – just feelings.

On reflection, I have at times through this been impatient, I knew what I wanted or rather knew what I did not want. Once I had made that decision, I wanted the change right there and then. My little friend hindsight tells me that I could have saved myself some tough days if I had waited to see things unfold. I now know that if things are meant for you, they will come to you, pushing and pulling is not right. You do not want to waste time on things that are not meant for you at this time.

Then there was just me. I finally have my peace. And all that she could see, was the other side of the mountain. Waiting for the completion to be finalised, moved out and into a storage unit Sunday. Glad to see the back of the house that became an empty vessel once filled by my family then one by one they left leaving just me. I enjoyed being on my own and having some space and time, however not in that house. I have desperately wanted to move on for some time now and the day has arrived.

The memories are not in that house they are firmly stored in my heart. I am now in-between leaving that house and moving into my new one so have decided not to spend this time anxious instead to enjoy what this break will bring. The joy of staying with my eldest and her family has been precious, I feel most at home there. My youngest is coming down for her nineteenth birthday, she once said to me when she grew up, she wanted to live in a hotel so… I am going to make that happen, even if it is for five nights. Let's have some carefree fun, feel as if this time is precious. Then on to stay with friends which will also be lovely.

Feeling surprisingly good, two and a half years to get to the top of the mountain, all I wished for is becoming reality, almost surreal. So much to do now, creating my space is so important.

11 December, 2019

Is there no end to this long tiring road, I feel that I have done everything I could to mend all that needed mending? I have been positive, worked hard, made sure I was doing all I could then bang... It feels like I have fallen and there is a part of me that does not want to get up and fight any more.

"You're nearly there." If anyone else says that I may want to punch them. Nearly there?! Two and a half fucking years of "nearly being there". Not feeling sure this is all worth it. No, I did the right thing but now angry at the world. Stupid for thinking this might get easier at some time.

Failure, that is me. That is how I feel. I tried and failed. Not a clue which way to turn, or what I am going to do.

The sad thing is I felt so happy the last couple of days, staying with my daughter and her family, I was at home. Looking forward to having them with me in my home. Making things with the children and getting back to a settled life. I have so much I wanted to do without the hassle of lawyers and estate agents.

Waking up with the feeling that everything is now in alignment, I am finally in the right place at the right time. I have created my new world, my space where I can just be me and for the first time put myself first without feeling guilty. I have never ever felt so at home, that surely cannot be about these four walls. This feeling is more than that, I got to where I was going to. All those sleepless nights are now fading away, I will never forget them, but I got to the next stage. However, this is not it, it's okay for now but this is just the beginning.

Successfully unfucked myself, no other way to put it. No, that does not mean I have turned into a finished product it just means that I am where I should be in life.

Good relationships, fulfilment, peace and a big slash of hope for what is coming my way.

Did all the work around manifestation work? I believe so, everything but the yellow Lamborghini turned up. I am still following my dreams, I got to the next stage in the game.

Anyone looking in may think you are not living anything extraordinary; they do not know what path I have taken to get here or what my dream was. Things money cannot buy… Inner peace, independence, life where I am in a responsive state.

Back in the 'believe in what you can create', this has been a three-year mental battle with self. The power of having choice is now prevalent in my everyday life as I have built the foundations. No matter what happens now, I have my base to work from and that is both physical and mental bases.

Where I am now was worth every dark day I experienced, might not have said that at the time!

Even my closed heart is wide open once more, defences are down. I am a long way from home… looking over my shoulder, my comfort has been taken away, I am exposed, standing alone with no familiarities, at my most vulnerable but at my most secure.

The tough road, no wonder I hid so long.

Opening the door to my new house, I have mentally and physically arrived at my peaceful place. I instantly feel at home, the most I have ever felt at home anywhere. Its Valentine's Day, a loving gift to myself, how very fitting. I can say it, I love myself and the new world I have created. On this day I realise a few things... I have truly learned to love myself... my creation of my space gives me the inner peace I so needed... this is not the end; I am starting again from the strongest position I have ever found myself in. Time to be braver, stronger more vulnerable and reminding myself about living in the moment. what is coming to you will show up, my impatience has only caused me anguish.

I talk about 'My Space' a lot now. This is my creation, it has taken three and a half years of determination and a vision based on HOPE, nothing more. I turned my back on my husband, my family, my home, my future and security, friends (so called) and a way of life that I had adopted. So, when I talk about 'My Space' it is my place of congruence, peace, my happy place, please do not enter if you have nothing good to bring me as I will now protect this space fiercely.

So that's my story... What is yours?